19/06

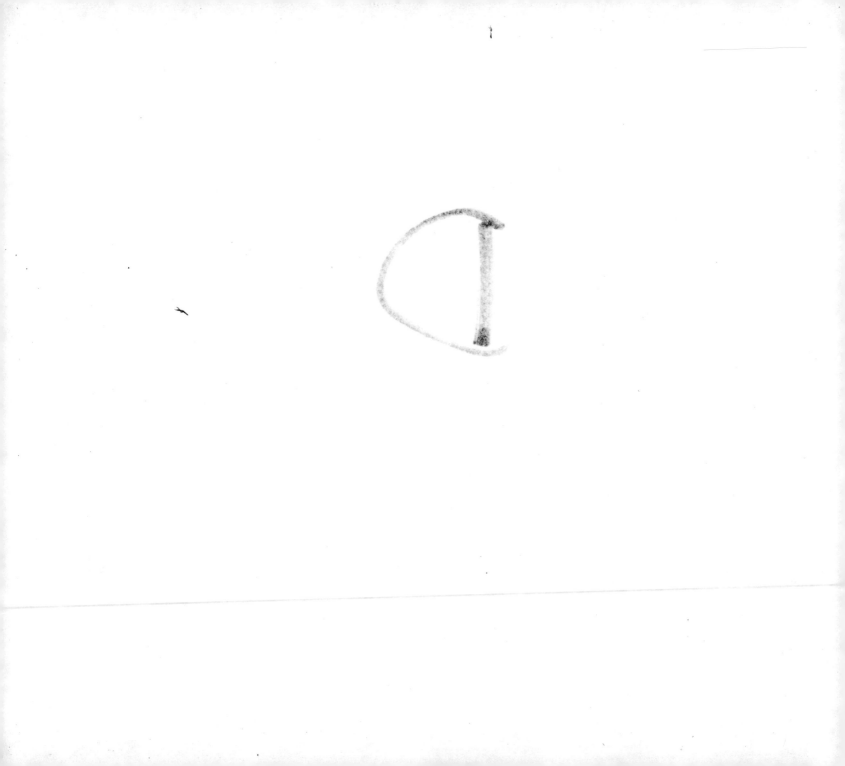

WELCOME TO THE U.S.A.

UTAH

Written by Ann Heinrichs   Illustrated by Matt Kania
Content Adviser: Bonnie Rogers Miller, Education Specialist,
Utah State Historical Society, Salt Lake City, Utah

The Child's World

Published in the United States of America by The Child's World®
PO Box 326 • Chanhassen, MN 55317-0326
800-599-READ • www.childsworld.com

Photo Credits
Cover: Getty Images/Photographer's Choice/Gavin Hellier; frontispiece: Medioimages.

Interior: AP/Wide World Photos: 10 (Douglas C. Pizac), 26 (Standard-Examiner/Tim Schoon); Brand X Pictures: 34; Corbis: 9 (Lee Cohen), 13 (Galen Rowell), 18 (Kevin Fleming), 21 (Scott T. Smith), 22 (Bruce Burkhardt), 25 (Dave G. Houser); Getty Images/The Image Bank/Nick Nicholson: 33; Hill Aerospace Museum: 30; George H. H. Huey/Corbis: 6, 14; Kencraft Candies: 29; Valerie Taylor: 17.

Acknowledgments
The Child's World®: Mary Berendes, Publishing Director

Editorial Directions, Inc.: E. Russell Primm, Editorial Director; Katie Marsico, Associate Editor; Judith Shiffer, Assistant Editor; Matt Messbarger, Editorial Assistant; Susan Hindman, Copy Editor; Melissa McDaniel, Proofreader; Kevin Cunningham, Peter Garnham, Matt Messbarger, Olivia Nellums, Chris Simms, Molly Symmonds, Katherine Trickle, Carl Stephen Wender, Fact Checkers; Tim Griffin/IndexServ, Indexer; Cian Loughlin O'Day, Photo Researcher and Editor

The Design Lab: Kathleen Petelinsek, Design; Julia Goozen, Art Production

Library of Congress Cataloging-in-Publication Data
Heinrichs, Ann.
  Utah / by Ann Heinrichs ; cartography and illustrations by Matt Kania.
    p. cm. — (Welcome to the U.S.A.)
  Includes index.
  ISBN 1-59296-486-9 (library bound : alk. paper) 1. Utah—Juvenile literature.
I. Kania, Matt, ill. II. Title.
F826.3.H453 2006
979.2—dc22   2005008821

Ann Heinrichs is the author of more than 100 books for children and young adults. She has also enjoyed successful careers as a children's book editor and an advertising copywriter. Ann grew up in Fort Smith, Arkansas, and lives in Chicago, Illinois.

About the Author Ann Heinrichs

Matt Kania loves maps and, as a kid, dreamed of making them. In school he studied geography and cartography, and today he makes maps for a living. Matt's favorite thing about drawing maps is learning about the places they represent. Many of the maps he has created can be found in books, magazines, videos, Web sites, and public places.

About the Map Illustrator Matt Kania

On the cover: Discover Utah's beautiful landscape at Canyonlands National Park.
On page one: The Mormon Temple lights up the night in Salt Lake City.

OUR UTAH TRIP

Utah's Nickname:
The Beehive State

Are you ready to tour the Beehive State? That's Utah. You'll be busy as a bee on this trip! Just wait and see.

You'll hike through deep **canyons.** You'll float in a lake and never sink. You'll learn about **pioneers** and railroads. You'll watch miners dig copper from the ground. You'll tour a candy factory and eat roasted lamb. And you'll see some ancient rock art!

There's a lot to do, so let's get going. Just buckle up and hang on tight. Utah, here we come!

WELCOME TO
UTAH

As you travel through Utah, watch for all the interesting facts along the way.

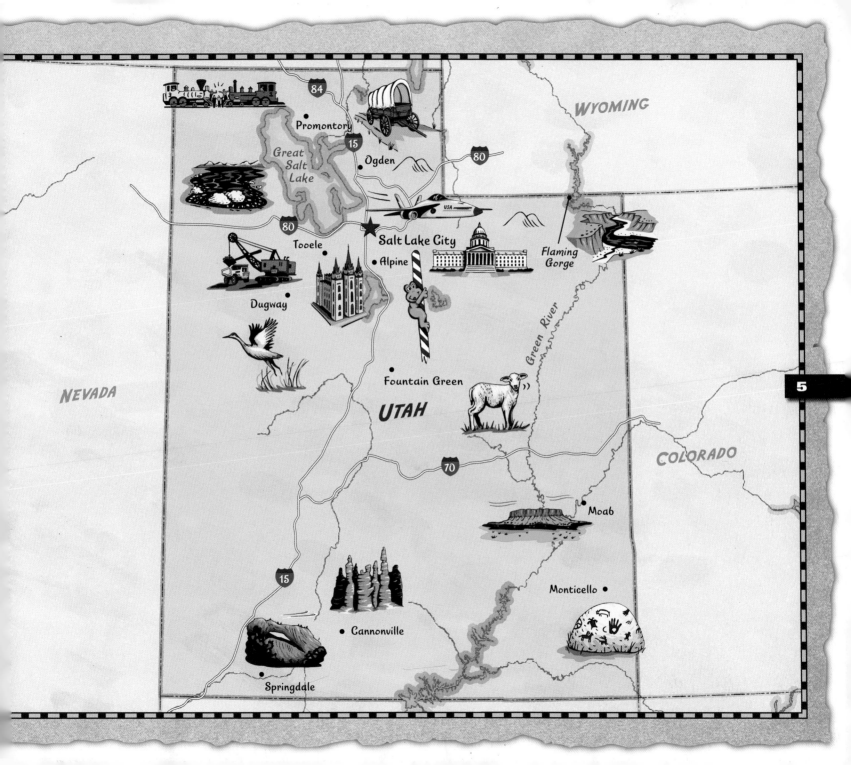

Promontory

Great
Salt
Lake

Ogden

WYOMING

84

15

80

Tooele

Salt Lake City

Alpine

Flaming
Gorge

Dugway

80

NEVADA

Fountain Green

Green River

UTAH

5

COLORADO

70

Moab

15

Monticello

Cannonville

Springdale

What amazing shapes! Don't forget to visit Bryce Canyon!

Paiute Indians called the Bryce Canyon rock formations "Legend People."

Thousands of weirdly shaped rocks loom overhead. They're called hoodoos or goblin rocks. You're exploring Bryce Canyon National Park! It's in southern Utah, near Cannonville.

Utah has many strange, colorful rock formations. Wind and water carved them over the years. The Rocky Mountains cover much of the state. Some mountains are snowcapped all year long.

The Green River runs through eastern Utah. It joins the Colorado River near Moab. Western Utah is very dry. The Great Salt Lake is in the northwest. Nearby is the Great Salt Lake Desert. Its surface is as hard as rock!

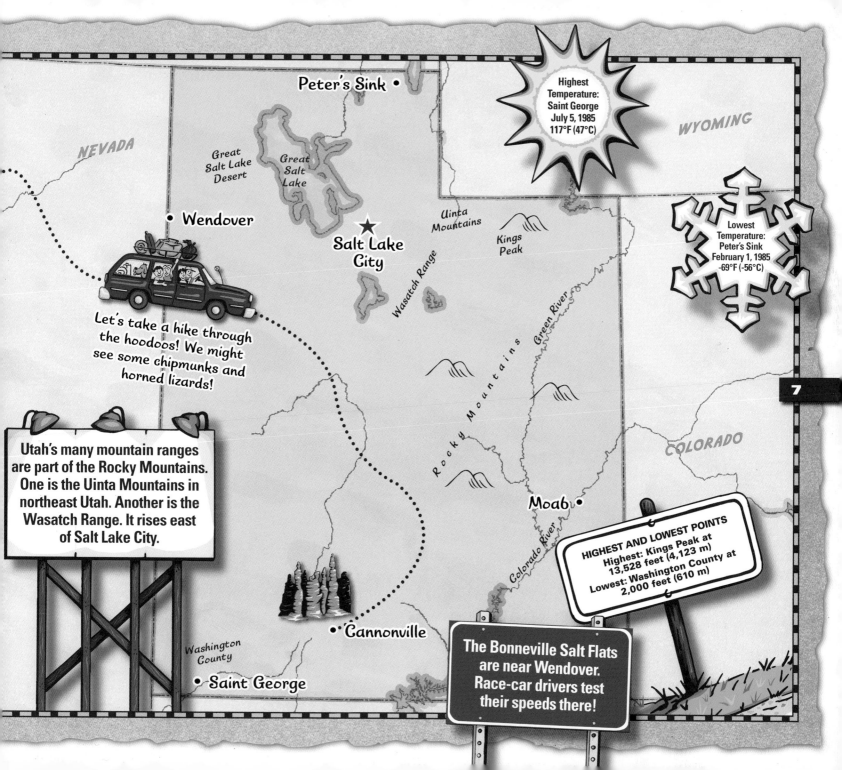

Peter's Sink •

Highest Temperature: Saint George July 5, 1985 117°F (47°C)

WYOMING

NEVADA

Great Salt Lake Desert

Great Salt Lake

• Wendover

Lowest Temperature: Peter's Sink February 1, 1985 -69°F (-56°C)

Uinta Mountains

★ Salt Lake City

Kings Peak

Wasatch Range

Let's take a hike through the hoodoos! We might see some chipmunks and horned lizards!

Green River

Rocky Mountains

COLORADO

Utah's many mountain ranges are part of the Rocky Mountains. One is the Uinta Mountains in northeast Utah. Another is the Wasatch Range. It rises east of Salt Lake City.

Moab •

Colorado River

HIGHEST AND LOWEST POINTS
Highest: Kings Peak at 13,528 feet (4,123 m)
Lowest: Washington County at 2,000 feet (610 m)

• Cannonville

Washington County

The Bonneville Salt Flats are near Wendover. Race-car drivers test their speeds there!

• Saint George

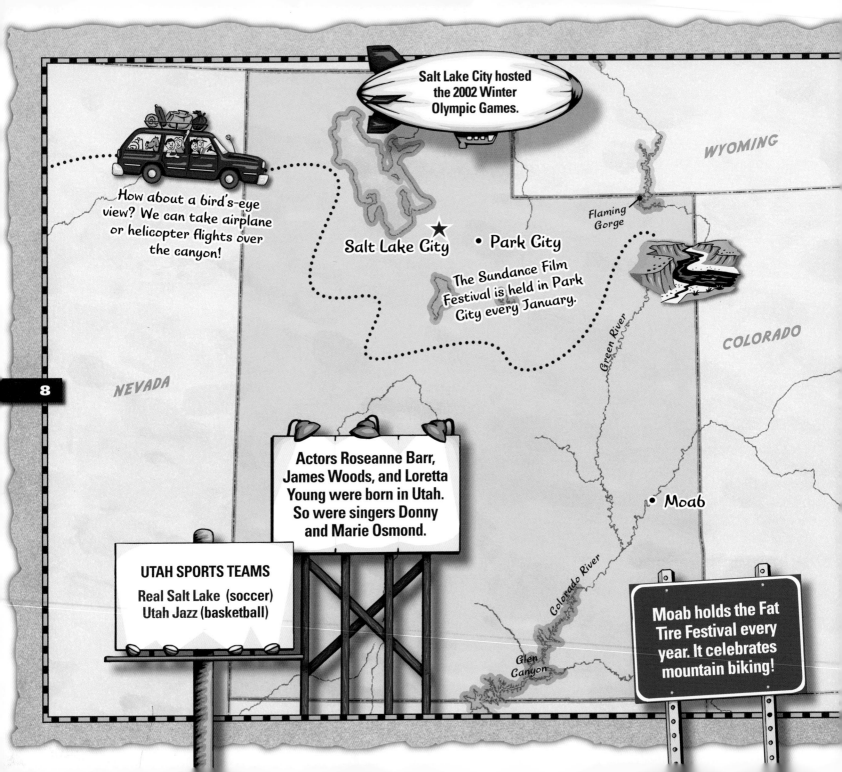

Salt Lake City hosted the 2002 Winter Olympic Games.

WYOMING

How about a bird's-eye view? We can take airplane or helicopter flights over the canyon!

Flaming Gorge

★ Salt Lake City • Park City

The Sundance Film Festival is held in Park City every January.

COLORADO

Green River

NEVADA

• Moab

Actors Roseanne Barr, James Woods, and Loretta Young were born in Utah. So were singers Donny and Marie Osmond.

UTAH SPORTS TEAMS

Real Salt Lake (soccer)
Utah Jazz (basketball)

Colorado River

Glen Canyon

Moab holds the Fat Tire Festival every year. It celebrates mountain biking!

Fun in Flaming Gorge

Don't forget your life jacket! Visitors paddle through Flaming Gorge.

There's so much to do in Flaming Gorge! Swoosh down the lake in a canoe. Brightly colored canyon walls rise around you. Explore the rock walls on foot. You'll see ancient Indian rock art. Or hike the Canyon Rim Trail. You'll spot wildlife among the red-rock mountains.

There's plenty to do outdoors in Utah. People enjoy boating, fishing, hiking, rock climbing, and skiing. Flaming Gorge and Glen Canyon are popular spots. Do you like bike riding? Then try mountain biking!

Flaming Gorge stretches across the Utah–Wyoming border. Its **reservoir** was created by a dam on the Green River.

Wildlife at Fish Springs

This heron calls Fish Springs home.

You see herons, egrets, rails, and cranes. These long-legged birds wade in the water. They catch fish and gulp them down!

You're visiting Fish Springs National Wildlife **Refuge.** Deserts are all around this refuge. But the refuge itself is a wetland. It gets its water from underground springs.

Thousands of birds nest and feed here. There are ducks, geese, eagles, and owls. Lots of other animals live in the area. They include coyotes, jackrabbits, antelopes, and mule deer.

Cactuses and other hardy plants grow in Utah's deserts. Forests cover some of the mountains. But watch out! Bears and mountain lions hide out there.

10

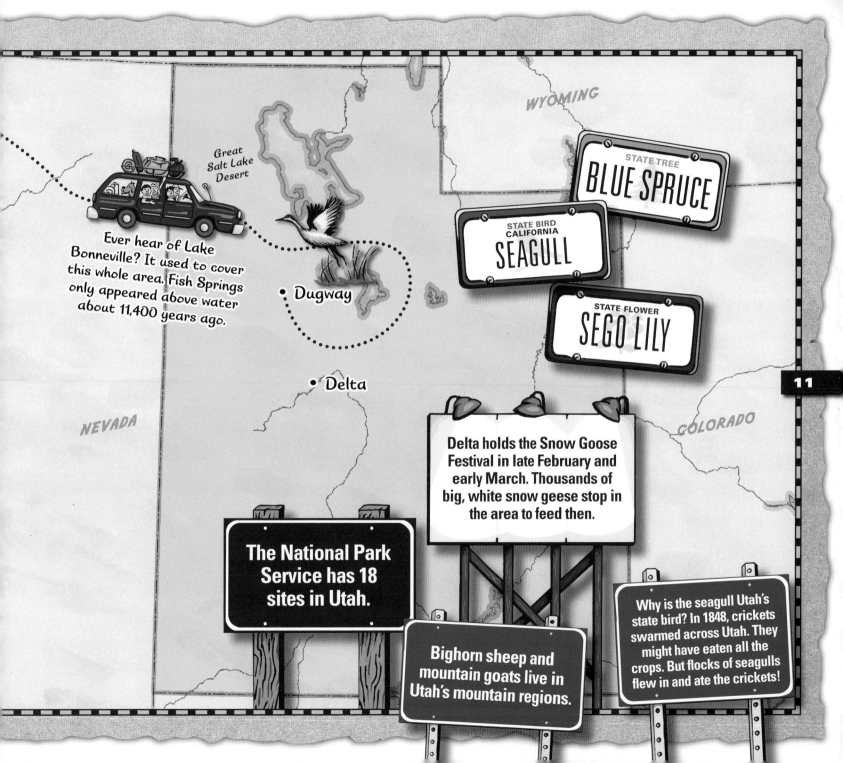

Great Salt Lake Desert

Ever hear of Lake Bonneville? It used to cover this whole area. Fish Springs only appeared above water about 11,400 years ago.

• Dugway

• Delta

NEVADA

WYOMING

STATE TREE
BLUE SPRUCE

STATE BIRD
CALIFORNIA
SEAGULL

STATE FLOWER
SEGO LILY

COLORADO

Delta holds the Snow Goose Festival in late February and early March. Thousands of big, white snow geese stop in the area to feed then.

The National Park Service has 18 sites in Utah.

Bighorn sheep and mountain goats live in Utah's mountain regions.

Why is the seagull Utah's state bird? In 1848, crickets swarmed across Utah. They might have eaten all the crops. But flocks of seagulls flew in and ate the crickets!

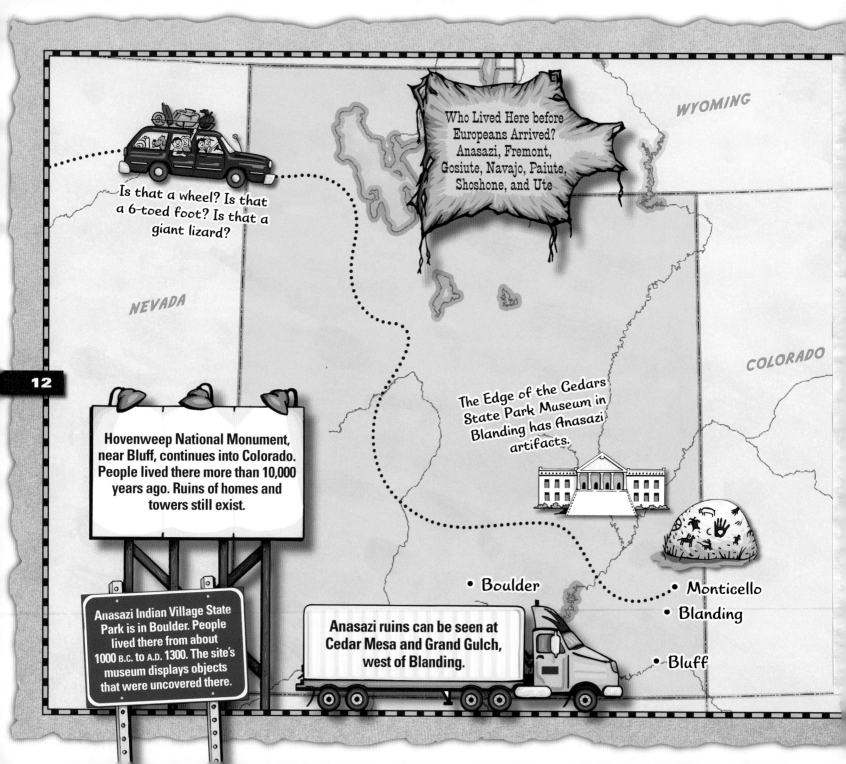

Is that a wheel? Is that a 6-toed foot? Is that a giant lizard?

Who Lived Here before Europeans Arrived? Anasazi, Fremont, Gosiute, Navajo, Paiute, Shoshone, and Ute

WYOMING

NEVADA

COLORADO

The Edge of the Cedars State Park Museum in Blanding has Anasazi artifacts.

Hovenweep National Monument, near Bluff, continues into Colorado. People lived there more than 10,000 years ago. Ruins of homes and towers still exist.

Anasazi Indian Village State Park is in Boulder. People lived there from about 1000 B.C. to A.D. 1300. The site's museum displays objects that were uncovered there.

Anasazi ruins can be seen at Cedar Mesa and Grand Gulch, west of Blanding.

• Boulder

• Monticello

• Blanding

• Bluff

Newspaper Rock near Monticello

Can you read Newspaper Rock? It's covered with pictures, not words. There are people, animals, and strange objects. They're petroglyphs, or art carved into rock. Ancient people carved them hundreds of years ago. The pictures are like a newspaper. They tell about many events and activities.

The Anasazi people carved most of these pictures. The Anasazi once lived in southern Utah. Some built homes high on the rock cliffs. Others built pueblos, or villages, many stories high. The Fremont people were another early group. Their homes were pits dug into the ground.

Do you look at pictures in the newspaper? Check out the ancient drawings at Newspaper Rock.

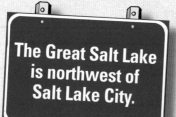

Take a moment to relax! Try floating
in the Great Salt Lake.

The Great Salt Lake
is northwest of
Salt Lake City.

The Great Salt Lake

Float in the lake without fear. You won't sink! But try not to swallow the water. It's so salty that you might choke. It's the Great Salt Lake!

Lake Bonneville once covered much of Utah. Its water dried up, leaving minerals called salts behind. The Great Salt Lake is the remains of Lake Bonneville. And it's very salty! It's even saltier than the ocean.

Jim Bridger reached the lake in 1824. He was probably the first white person there. Bridger tasted the salty water. He thought he'd reached the Pacific Ocean!

Bridger was a fur trapper and scout. Many other trappers soon arrived in Utah.

Spanish explorers reached Utah in 1765. But they did not establish towns there.

WYOMING

Great Salt Lake

★ Salt Lake City

Let's jump in the north side of the lake! We'll float better there. It's twice as salty as the south side.

The salt we eat with our food is sodium chloride. Some companies gather salt from the Great Salt Lake and later use it to make sodium chloride.

NEVADA

COLORADO

Salt companies take water from the Great Salt Lake. They process the water to make dry salt. Some of that salt is used on icy roads in winter.

The saltier the lake's water is, the better things float in it. After a big rain, things don't float as well. That's because the lake has more water and less salt.

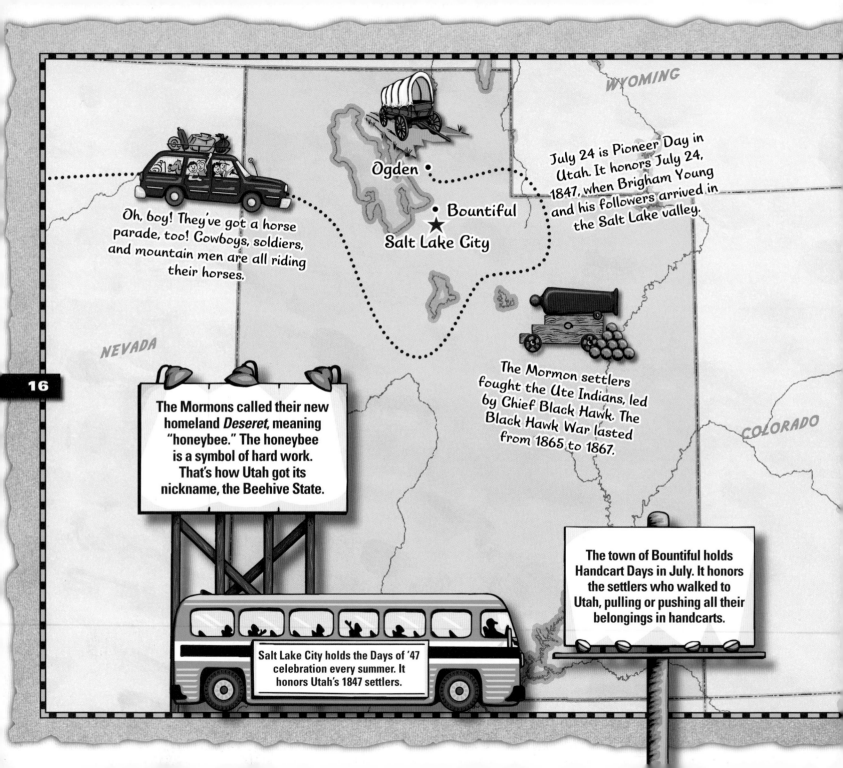

WYOMING

NEVADA

COLORADO

Ogden

Bountiful

Salt Lake City

Oh, boy! They've got a horse parade, too! Cowboys, soldiers, and mountain men are all riding their horses.

July 24 is Pioneer Day in Utah. It honors July 24, 1847, when Brigham Young and his followers arrived in the Salt Lake valley.

The Mormons called their new homeland *Deseret*, meaning "honeybee." The honeybee is a symbol of hard work. That's how Utah got its nickname, the Beehive State.

The Mormon settlers fought the Ute Indians, led by Chief Black Hawk. The Black Hawk War lasted from 1865 to 1867.

The town of Bountiful holds Handcart Days in July. It honors the settlers who walked to Utah, pulling or pushing all their belongings in handcarts.

Salt Lake City holds the Days of '47 celebration every summer. It honors Utah's 1847 settlers.

Pioneer Days in Ogden

Kids are marching with decorated wagons and bikes. Covered wagons are rolling along. It's the Pioneer Days parade in Ogden!

Pioneer Days celebrates Utah's first white settlers. Brigham Young led them there in 1847. They all belonged to the Mormon religion. They were seeking religious freedom.

Most of the settlers had traveled from Illinois. It was a long, hard journey. They walked with handcarts or rode in covered wagons. By 1869, about 70,000 Mormons were in Utah. They built **irrigation** systems across the dry land. Then they could grow many crops.

Giddyup! This rider is part of the Pioneer Days parade.

Utah is named after the Ute Indians who lived in the area.

Salt Lake City's Temple Square

Want to learn about the Mormon religion? Visit the beautiful Temple Square and see the Mormon Temple.

Joseph Smith (1805–1844) was the founder of Mormonism. He published the Book of Mormon in 1830. This is the holy book of the Mormon faith.

You cannot miss Temple Square. It's Salt Lake City's most famous site. The Mormon Temple stands at one end. It's a beautiful house of worship. The public may not go inside, though.

Nearby is the Mormon Tabernacle. Its organ and choir are world famous. Also in Temple Square is the Beehive House. Brigham Young lived there in the 1800s.

Many more buildings stand in Temple Square. They all relate to Mormon history and activities. Salt Lake City is the Mormon church's world center. Today, the Mormon faith is strong in Utah. About seven out of ten residents are Mormons.

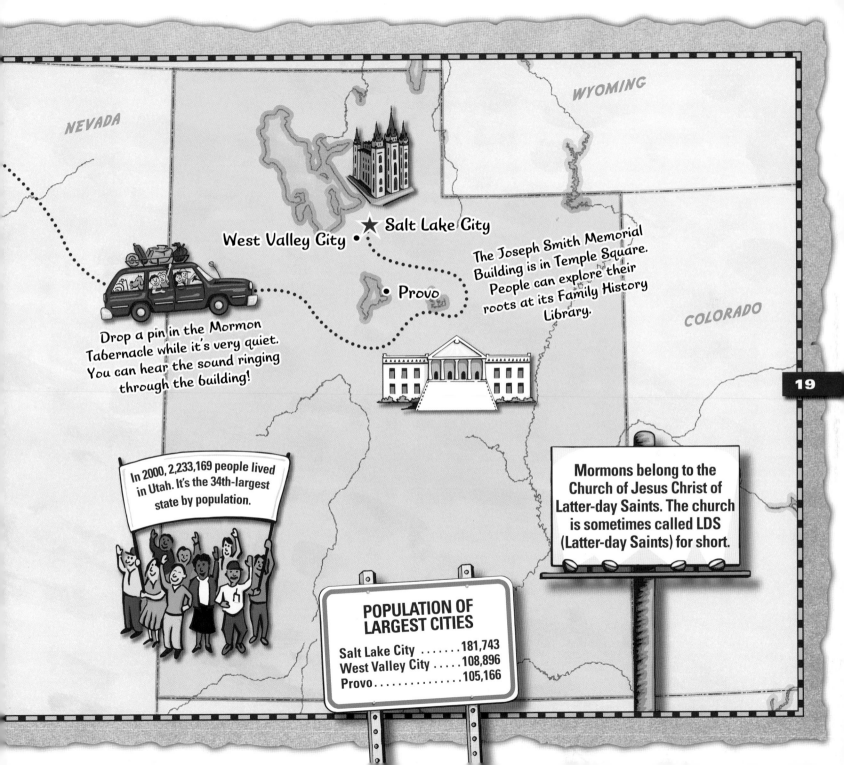

NEVER

WYOMING

NEVADA

★ Salt Lake City

West Valley City •

• Provo

COLORADO

The Joseph Smith Memorial Building is in Temple Square. People can explore their roots at its Family History Library.

Drop a pin in the Mormon Tabernacle while it's very quiet. You can hear the sound ringing through the building!

In 2000, 2,233,169 people lived in Utah. It's the 34th-largest state by population.

Mormons belong to the Church of Jesus Christ of Latter-day Saints. The church is sometimes called LDS (Latter-day Saints) for short.

POPULATION OF LARGEST CITIES

Salt Lake City 181,743
West Valley City 108,896
Provo 105,166

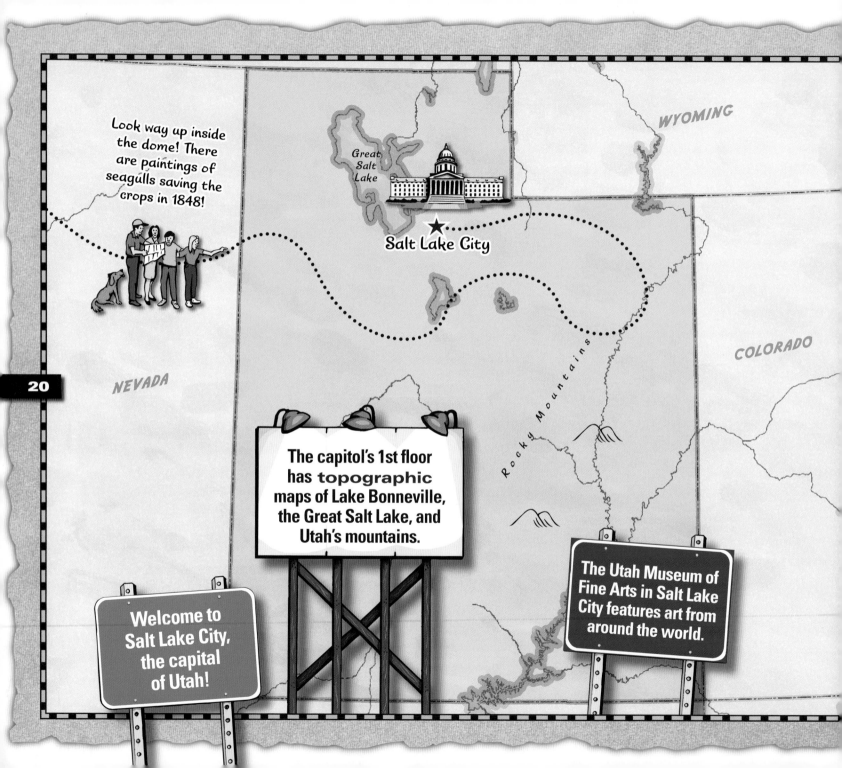

Look way up inside the dome! There are paintings of seagulls saving the crops in 1848!

WYOMING

Great Salt Lake

★
Salt Lake City

NEVADA

COLORADO

Rocky Mountains

The capitol's 1st floor has **topographic** maps of Lake Bonneville, the Great Salt Lake, and Utah's mountains.

The Utah Museum of Fine Arts in Salt Lake City features art from around the world.

Welcome to Salt Lake City, the capital of Utah!

Utah's state motto is "Industry."

Is history your favorite subject? Head to Utah's capitol! You'll learn a lot about the rotunda.

Utah's state capitol is full of history lessons. The lessons are all in pictures! Just stand in the rotunda. That's the tall, rounded space under the dome. The wall paintings show historical scenes. They include many early explorers. And you'll see Brigham Young and his pioneers.

This building houses Utah's state government offices. Utah has three branches of government. One branch consists of the state lawmakers. Another branch makes sure laws are carried out. The governor heads this branch. The third branch is made up of courts. Judges rule over the courts. They decide whether laws have been broken.

21

Hike along the cliffs at Zion National Park. Don't look down if you're afraid of heights!

Kolob Arch measures more than 290 feet (88 m) across.

Exploring Zion National Park

Zion National Park is an awesome place. It's full of towering cliffs and deep canyons. Its rock formations are pink, red, and orange.

Mormons first settled this area in the 1860s. They gave it the Hebrew name *Zion*. That means "a place of safety and rest."

What can you do in Zion National Park? You can hike! Many people hike the Zion Narrows. Its towering rock walls are very close together. The park's Kolob **Arch** is a famous site. It may be the world's largest natural arch.

Do you like watching wildlife? You'll see lots of animals in the park. There are bighorn sheep and mountain lions. There are roadrunners, too!

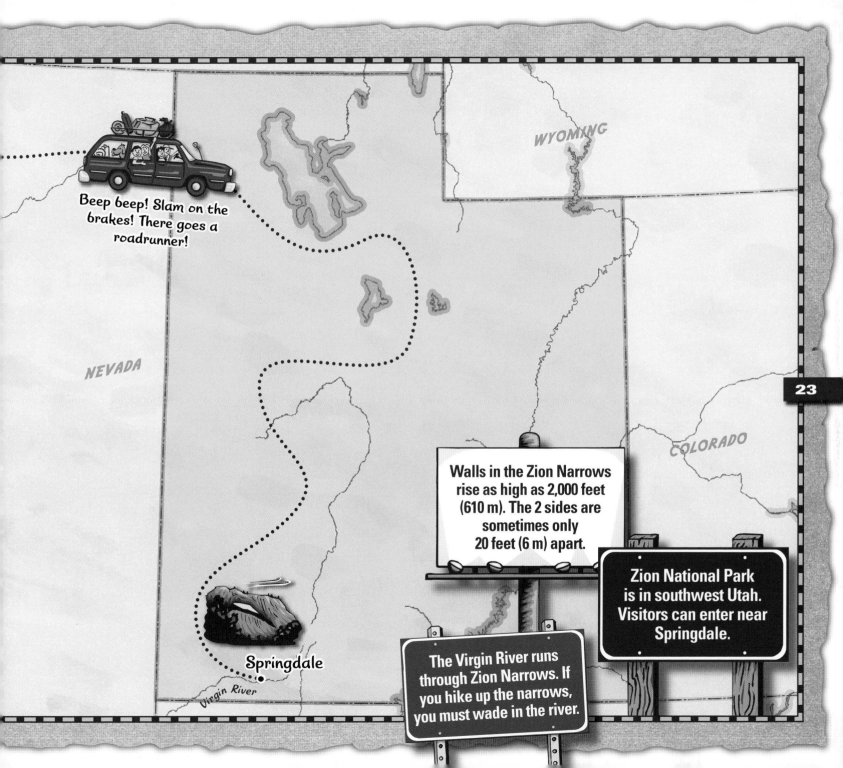

Beep beep! Slam on the brakes! There goes a roadrunner!

WYOMING

NEVADA

COLORADO

Walls in the Zion Narrows rise as high as 2,000 feet (610 m). The 2 sides are sometimes only 20 feet (6 m) apart.

Zion National Park is in southwest Utah. Visitors can enter near Springdale.

Springdale

Virgin River

The Virgin River runs through Zion Narrows. If you hike up the narrows, you must wade in the river.

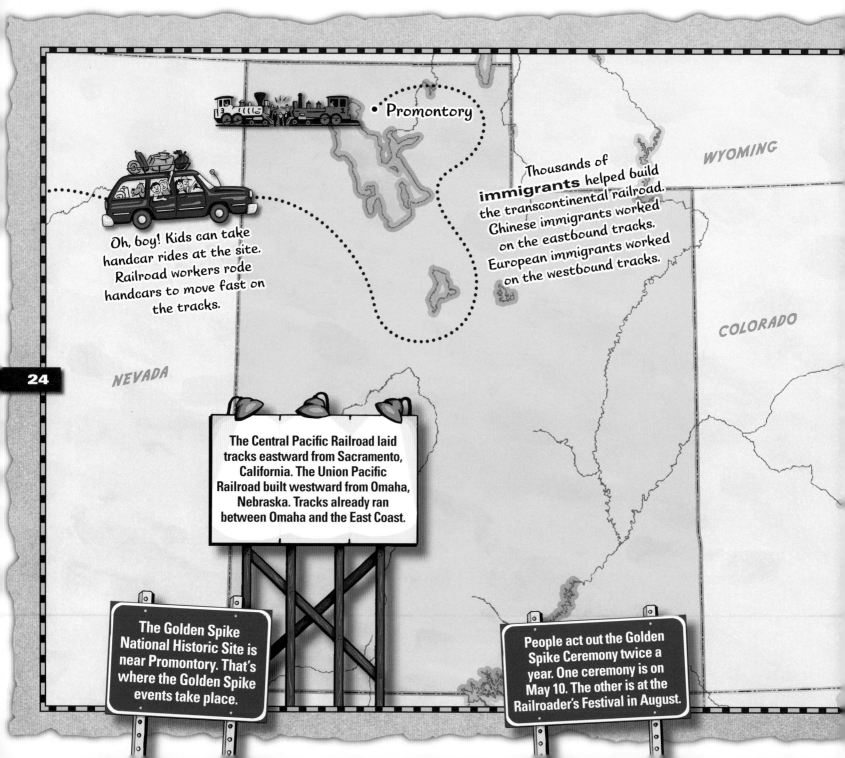

Oh, boy! Kids can take handcar rides at the site. Railroad workers rode handcars to move fast on the tracks.

• Promontory

Thousands of **immigrants** helped build the transcontinental railroad. Chinese immigrants worked on the eastbound tracks. European immigrants worked on the westbound tracks.

WYOMING

COLORADO

NEVADA

The Central Pacific Railroad laid tracks eastward from Sacramento, California. The Union Pacific Railroad built westward from Omaha, Nebraska. Tracks already ran between Omaha and the East Coast.

The Golden Spike National Historic Site is near Promontory. That's where the Golden Spike events take place.

People act out the Golden Spike Ceremony twice a year. One ceremony is on May 10. The other is at the Railroader's Festival in August.

Promontory's Golden Spike

The Golden Spike completed the transcontinental railroad on May 10, 1869.

Ching, ching! People are swinging enormous hammers. They're hammering gigantic **spikes.** What's going on?

It's the Golden Spike Ceremony! This event first took place in 1869. People act it out every year in Promontory.

The Golden Spike was a big, gold railroad spike. It joined the last section of the transcontinental railroad. The railroad stretched across the whole country.

Some workers built tracks heading west. Others built tracks heading east. The two sections met in Promontory. The Golden Spike was hammered in. Then everyone cheered!

All aboard! You can see trains from the 1800s in Promontory.

Ever wonder how copper is mined? Visit the Kennecott copper mine and find out!

The Kennecott copper pit is the world's largest hole dug by humans. Astronauts can even see it from space!

Visiting Kennecott Copper Mine

Look over the railing at Bingham Canyon. You're looking down into a massive pit. Huge trucks are hauling chunks of copper ore. They dump the **ore** into a crusher. It crushes the ore into smaller pieces. How small? About the size of soccer balls!

You're visiting the Kennecott copper mine near Tooele. Mining became a big **industry** in Utah. Southeastern Utah had rich coal deposits. Coal mines dotted this region in the 1880s. Other areas were known for their iron, silver, gold, and lead.

Copper mining became important in the 1890s. The Bingham Canyon area was rich in copper. It's one of the world's top copper producers today.

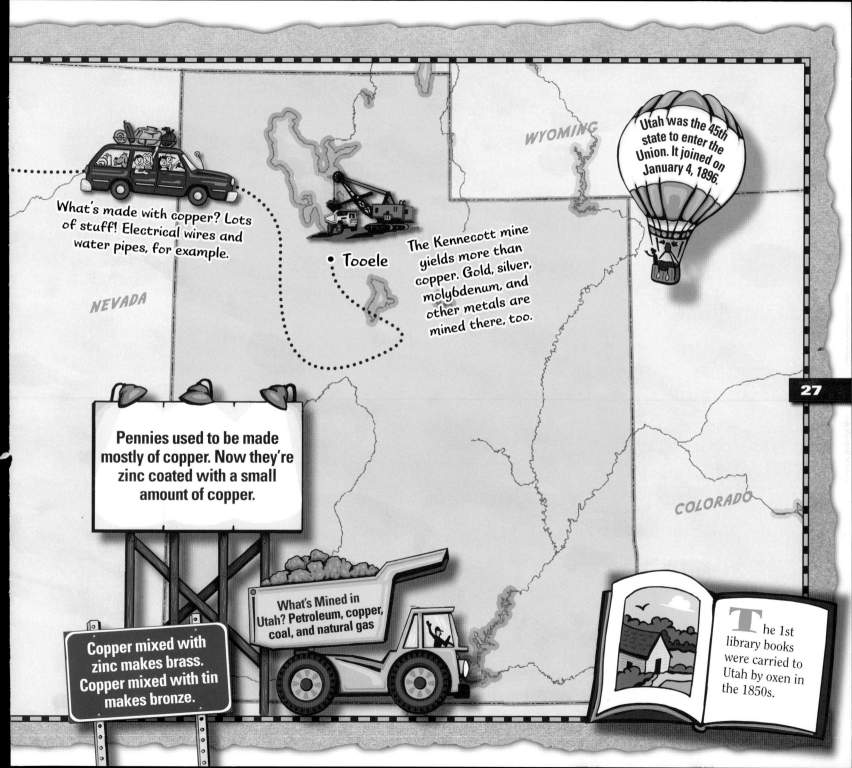

What's made with copper? Lots of stuff! Electrical wires and water pipes, for example.

NEVADA

WYOMING

• Tooele

The Kennecott mine yields more than copper. Gold, silver, molybdenum, and other metals are mined there, too.

Utah was the 45th state to enter the Union. It joined on January 4, 1896.

Pennies used to be made mostly of copper. Now they're zinc coated with a small amount of copper.

COLORADO

What's Mined in Utah? Petroleum, copper, coal, and natural gas

Copper mixed with zinc makes brass. Copper mixed with tin makes bronze.

The 1st library books were carried to Utah by oxen in the 1850s.

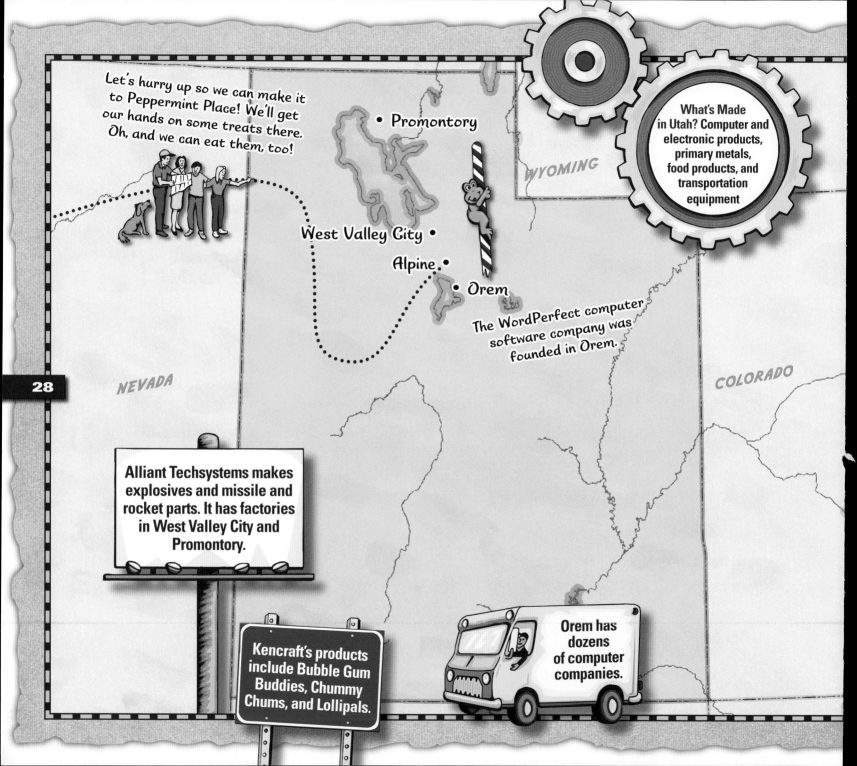

Let's hurry up so we can make it to Peppermint Place! We'll get our hands on some treats there. Oh, and we can eat them, too!

Promontory

WYOMING

What's Made in Utah? Computer and electronic products, primary metals, food products, and transportation equipment

West Valley City

Alpine

Orem

The WordPerfect computer software company was founded in Orem.

NEVADA

COLORADO

Alliant Techsystems makes explosives and missile and rocket parts. It has factories in West Valley City and Promontory.

Kencraft's products include Bubble Gum Buddies, Chummy Chums, and Lollipals.

Orem has dozens of computer companies.

Touring Kencraft Candies

Kettles are boiling the syrupy goo. Then workers put it into the stretching machine. Each gooey glob is bent, twisted, and cut. Next, watch the candy artists. They add decorations in sugary colors. What's the final product? Candy sticks, candy canes, and suckers—yum!

You're touring Kencraft. It's a candy factory in Alpine. Food products are among Utah's many factory goods. Some food plants make yummy snacks—like candy!

Metals and computers are also made in Utah. Some factories make parts for missiles and rockets. Others make air bags for cars. Medicines are Utah products, too.

Want to know how candy is made? Treat your sweet tooth at Kencraft.

Would you like to be a pilot? Take a tour of Hill Aerospace Museum!

Check out Hill **Aerospace** Museum. You'll see lots of military airplanes. Some have snarly faces painted on them!

This museum is on Hill Air Force Base. It's just south of Ogden. The aerospace industry is important in Utah.

Wendover Range was busy during World War II (1939–1945). Airplanes practiced dropping bombs there. Dugway Proving Ground opened in 1942. It's still a military testing site. In the 1950s, Utah began building missiles. Utah still makes parts for missiles, rockets, and spacecraft.

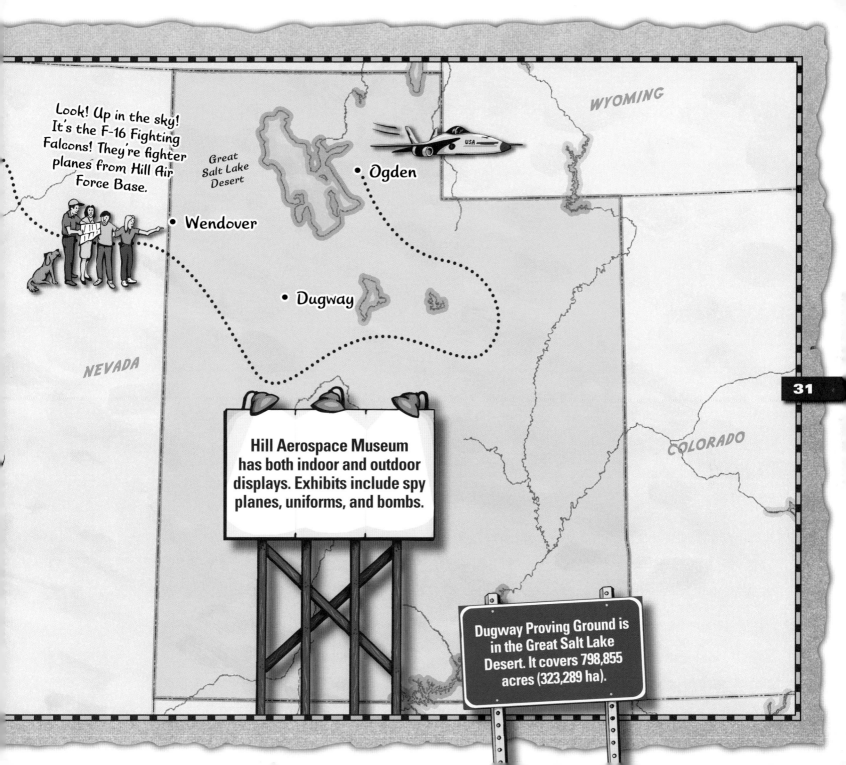

Look! Up in the sky! It's the F-16 Fighting Falcons! They're fighter planes from Hill Air Force Base.

WYOMING

Great Salt Lake Desert

• Ogden

USA

• Wendover

• Dugway

NEVADA

COLORADO

Hill Aerospace Museum has both indoor and outdoor displays. Exhibits include spy planes, uniforms, and bombs.

Dugway Proving Ground is in the Great Salt Lake Desert. It covers 798,855 acres (323,289 ha).

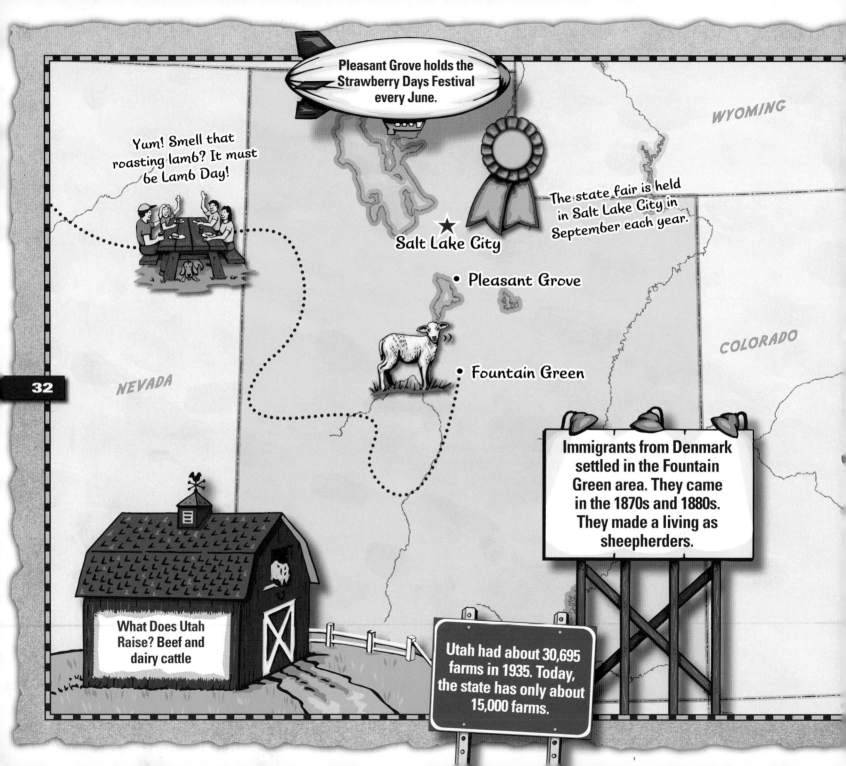

Pleasant Grove holds the Strawberry Days Festival every June.

WYOMING

Yum! Smell that roasting lamb? It must be Lamb Day!

The state fair is held in Salt Lake City in September each year.

★
Salt Lake City

• Pleasant Grove

COLORADO

• Fountain Green

NEVADA

Immigrants from Denmark settled in the Fountain Green area. They came in the 1870s and 1880s. They made a living as sheepherders.

What Does Utah Raise? Beef and dairy cattle

Utah had about 30,695 farms in 1935. Today, the state has only about 15,000 farms.

Lamb Day in Fountain Green

Kids are dressed as lambs for the parade. Lamb is roasting in big barbecue pits. People are racing in the Lamb Scram. It's Lamb Day!

Lamb Day is a big festival in Fountain Green. It celebrates the region's sheepherding history. Utah is a leading state for raising sheep. Beef and dairy cattle are valuable, too. They produce tons of meat and milk. Many farmers also raise hogs and chickens.

Hay is Utah's leading crop. Most of it is fed to cattle. Some farmers raise cherries, apples, strawberries, and peaches. These fruits make great desserts!

Baa! Many Utah farmers raise sheep.

Most of Utah's farmland is watered by irrigation.

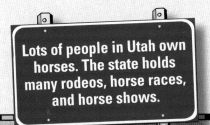

Lots of people in Utah own horses. The state holds many rodeos, horse races, and horse shows.

Even more cool rock formations? Absolutely—just head to Canyonlands National Park!

The Green River meets the Colorado River in Canyonlands National Park.

The Wonders of Canyonlands

What is the Island in the Sky? What are the Needles and the **Maze**? They're all rock formations in Canyonlands National Park. It's Utah's largest national park.

It took millions of years to form Canyonlands. Rivers washed through it. The Earth's crust shifted there, too. Layers of rock formed and washed away. What is left today? A jumble of fantastic rock formations!

The Island in the Sky is well named. Its colorful rocks rise high atop a **mesa.** The Needles are tall, pointy rocks. The Maze is a really wild area. Its canyons are like a rocky puzzle. Be careful, and don't get lost!

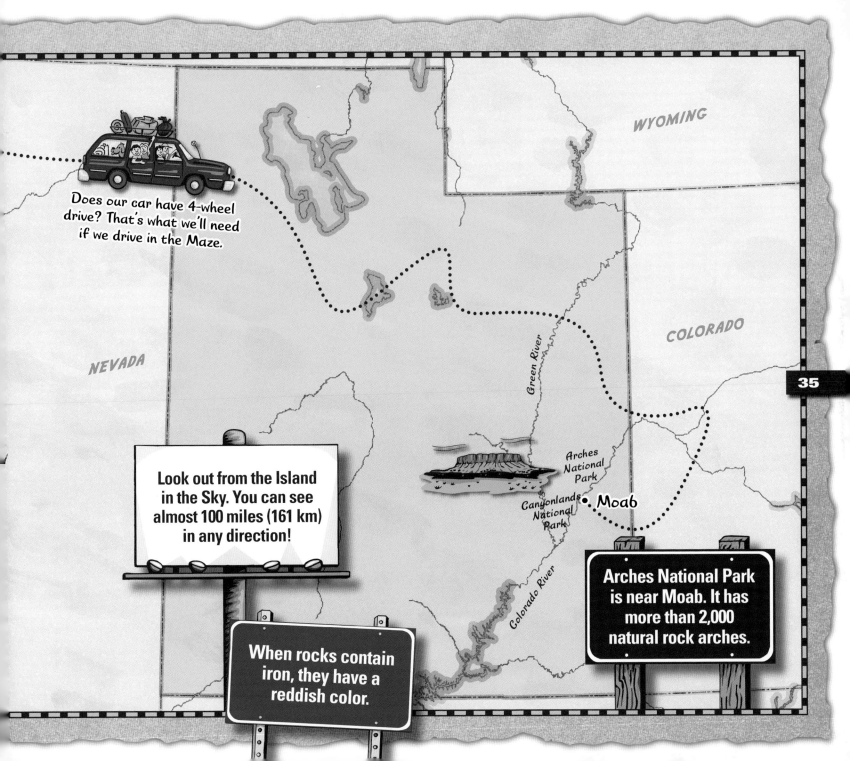

Does our car have 4-wheel drive? That's what we'll need if we drive in the Maze.

WYOMING

COLORADO

NEVADA

Green River

Arches National Park

Canyonlands National Park

• Moab

Look out from the Island in the Sky. You can see almost 100 miles (161 km) in any direction!

When rocks contain iron, they have a reddish color.

Colorado River

Arches National Park is near Moab. It has more than 2,000 natural rock arches.

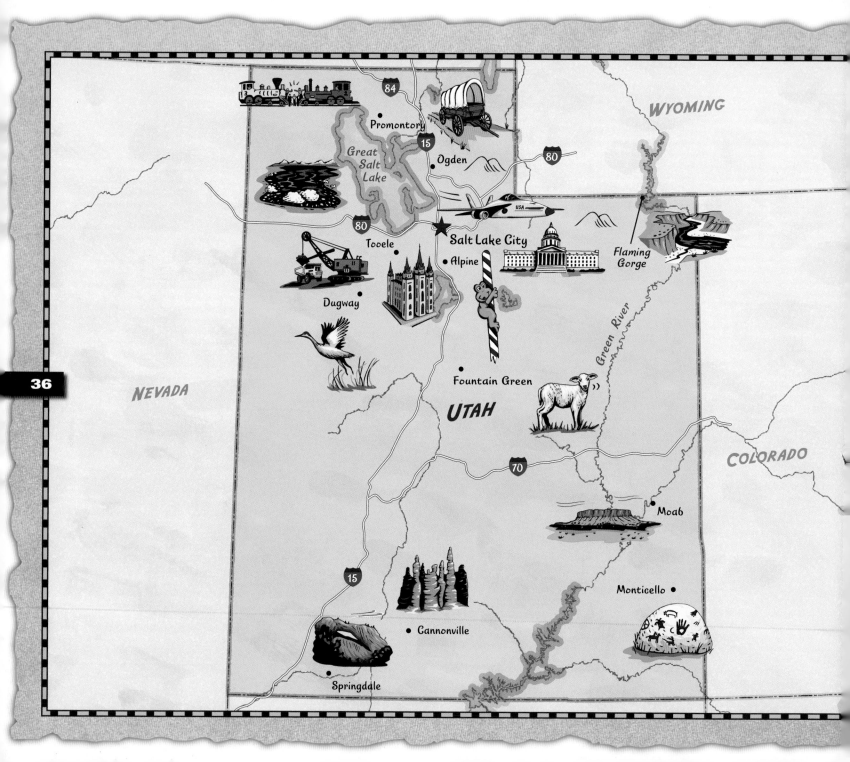

WYOMING

Promontory

84

15

Ogden

80

Great
Salt
Lake

USA

Tooele

80

Salt Lake City

Alpine

Flaming
Gorge

Dugway

Green River

NEVADA

Fountain Green

UTAH

COLORADO

70

Moab

15

Monticello

Cannonville

Springdale

OUR TRIP

We visited many amazing places on our trip! We also met a lot of interesting people along the way. Look at the map on your left. Use your finger to trace all the places we have been.

Where is the Sundance Film Festival held? See page 8 for the answer.

When did Fish Springs appear above water? Page 11 has the answer.

Where in Utah can Anasazi ruins be seen? See page 12 for the answer.

Who takes water from the Great Salt Lake? Look on page 15 for the answer.

Who was Joseph Smith? Page 18 has the answer.

What's on the 1st floor of Utah's capitol? Turn to page 20 for the answer.

What is copper mixed with zinc? Look on page 27 for the answer.

How many farms does Utah have? Turn to page 32 for the answer.

That was a great trip! We have traveled all over Utah. There are a few places that we didn't have time for, though. Next time, we plan to visit the Tracy Aviary in Salt Lake City. Visitors can see more than 135 kinds of birds there. They can even attend classes, shows, and camps to learn more about Utah's birds.

More Places to Visit in Utah

WORDS TO KNOW

aerospace (AIR-oh-spayss) relating to air and space flight

arch (ARCH) a curved structure above some sort of opening

canyons (KAN-yuhnz) deep valleys worn away by rivers

immigrants (IM-uh-gruhnts) people who leave their home country and move to another country

industry (IN-duh-stree) a type of business

irrigation (ihr-uh-GAY-shuhn) a human-made system of bringing water to farms through ditches

maze (MAYZ) a confusing network of pathways

mesa (MAY-suh) a high, flat-topped hill

ore (OR) rock that contains valuable materials such as iron or gold

pioneers (pye-uh-NEERZ) people who move to an unsettled land

refuge (REF-yooj) a place of safety and protection

reservoir (REZ-ur-vwar) a human-made lake

spikes (SPIKES) large, heavy nails used to fasten rails to railroad ties

topographic (top-uh-GRAF-ik) showing the physical features of land such as mountains and rivers

Utah covers 82,144 square miles (212,751 sq km). It's the 12th-largest state in size.

STATE SYMBOLS

State animal: Rocky Mountain elk

State bird: California seagull

State cooking pot: Dutch oven

State emblem: Beehive

State fish: Bonneville cutthroat trout

State flower: Sego lily

State folk dance: Square dance

State fossil: *Allosaurus*

State fruit: Cherry

State gem: Topaz

State grass: Indian rice grass

State historic vegetable: Sugar beet

State insect: Honeybee

State mineral: Copper

State rock: Coal

State star: Dubhe

State tree: Blue spruce

State vegetable: Spanish sweet onion

State flag

State seal

STATE SONG

"Utah . . . This Is the Place"

Words by Sam Francis and Gary Francis, music by Gary Francis

Utah! People working together
Utah! What a great place to be.
Blessed from Heaven above.
It's the land that we love.
This is the place!

Utah! With its mountains and valleys.
Utah! With its canyons and streams.
You can go anywhere.
But there's none that compare.
This is the place!

It was Brigham Young who led the pioneers across the plains.
They suffered with the trials they had to face.
With faith they kept on going till they reached the Great Salt Lake
Here they heard the words . . .
"THIS IS THE PLACE!"

Utah! With its focus on family,
Utah! Helps each child to succeed.
People care how they live.
Each has so much to give.
This is the place!

Utah! Getting bigger and better.
Utah! Always leading the way.
New technology's here . . .
Growing faster each year.
This is the place!

There is beauty in the snow-capped mountains, in the lakes and streams.
There are valleys filled with farms and orchards too.
The spirit of its people shows in everything they do.
Utah is the place where dreams come true.

Utah! With its pioneer spirit.
Utah! What a great legacy!
Blessed from Heaven above.
It's the land that we love.
This is the place!

Utah! Utah! Utah!
THIS IS THE PLACE!

FAMOUS PEOPLE

Barr, Roseanne (1952–), comedian and actor

Brimley, Wilford (1934–), actor

Cannon, Martha Hughes (1857–1932), 1st female state senator

Cassidy, Butch (1866–ca. 1908), outlaw who may have faked his death

Farnsworth, Philo (1906–1971), inventor

Fullmer, Gene (1931–), boxer

Garn, Jake (1932–), senator who became the 1st U.S. official to fly in space while in office

Malone, Karl (1963–), basketball player

Ogden, Peter Skene (1794–1854), fur trader and explorer

Osmond, Donny (1957–), singer and entertainer

Osmond, Marie (1959–), singer and entertainer

Redford, Robert (1937–), actor and director

Stegner, Wallace (1909–1993), author

Stockton, John (1962–), basketball player

Wakara (ca. 1815–1855), American Indian leader

Wells, Emmeline (1828–1921), Mormon leader and feminist

Woods, James (1947–), actor

Young, Brigham (1801–1877), Mormon leader

Young, Loretta (1913–2000), actor

Young, Steve (1961–), football player

TO FIND OUT MORE

At the Library
Dean, Arlan. *The Mormon Pioneer Trail: From Nauvoo, Illinois to the Great Salt Lake, Utah.* New York: PowerKids Press, 2003.

Hall, Rebecca, and Katherine Larson. *A Is for Arches: A Utah Alphabet.* Chelsea, Mich.: Sleeping Bear Press, 2003.

McCully, Emily Arnold. *An Outlaw Thanksgiving.* New York: Dial Books for Young Readers, 1998.

Petersen, David. *Zion National Park.* Chicago: Children's Press, 1993.

Stevens, Janet. *Coyote Steals the Blanket: A Ute Tale.* New York: Holiday House, 1993.

On the Web
Visit our home page for lots of links about Utah:
http://www.childsworld.com/links

Note to Parents, Teachers, and Librarians: We routinely verify our Web links to make sure they are safe, active sites—so encourage your readers to check them out!

Places to Visit or Contact
Utah State Historical Society
300 South Rio Grande Street
Salt Lake City, UT 84101
801/533-3500
For more information about the history of Utah

Utah Travel Council
300 N. State Street
Salt Lake City, UT 84114
801/538-1030
For more information about traveling in Utah

INDEX

Bye, Beehive State.
We had a great time.
We'll come back soon!